Want to know
the world

The North Pole and the South Pole

Pierre Winters & Margot Senden

Clavis

NEW YORK

It's such fun to play in the snow. Every winter it gets cold and then it snows. Sometimes there's just a little snow, sometimes there's a lot. You can throw snowballs or make a beautiful snowman. You can go sledding, ice skating or skiing. There's so much to do in the snow.

Imagine what it would be like if it was always icy and snowy and if it was always very cold. That's what it's like at the North Pole and the South Pole.

What are poles?

The earth is round like a ball. The ball is warmest on the sides, because that's where the sun is closest to the earth. The top and the bottom of the ball are cold. Those are the poles. The North pole is at the top and the South Pole is at the bottom of the ball. At both poles it is frozen all the time. This means that the temperature is below 32° Fahrenheit. Water turns into ice and no plants can grow. It's also difficult for humans to live in environments that are so cold.

Did you know
it is always light in summer
and dark in winter
at the poles?

What does the North Pole look like?

puffins

arctic tern

walrus

seals

polar bears

The North Pole consists only of ice. There is no earth underneath it, only water. It is a huge frozen sea. In summer it is 50° Fahrenheit and in winter the temperature can drop to -22° Fahrenheit.

water

ice

narwhal

dolphin

fulmar

reindeer

Did you know it almost never snows at the poles?

rabbit

arctic fox

lemming

The animals that live in the sea are the ones that can bear the cold water – whales, narwhals, and all sorts of ice fish. Polar bears, seals, sea lions, walruses, arctic foxes and lemmings live on the ice. There are also a lot of birds: fulmars, puffins, and all sorts of gulls. Birds need land to build nests and lay eggs. Around the frozen sea we call the North Pole, there is land: Lapland, Siberia and Greenland. It's often very cold there too.

What does the South Pole look like?

antarctic skua

fur seal

orcas

antarctic icefish

whale

krill

penguins

ice

land

Underneath the ice at the South Pole there is land. There, it is even colder than at the North Pole. In winter the temperature sometimes drops to -128° Fahrenheit. It's so cold that humans can't really live there. Whales and seals live in the sea around the South Pole. Penguins live there as well.

Did you know
the South Pole is also
called Antarctica?

So much ice!

At the poles there is a lot of ice.
At the North Pole it's frozen
seawater. In the middle of the
poles there is an ice cap of very
thick, solid ice that never melts.
At the side of the ice cap glaciers
are formed. Glaciers are large masses
of snow that build up over the years.
Every winter they grow and every summer
they melt a bit, but they usually grow more
than they melt. When a chunk of glacier
breaks off and floats into the water it's
called an iceberg. The biggest part of an
iceberg is hidden under water. You can
only see the very top. Animals live on the
icebergs. In the summer when it melts,
big chunks of ice and snow can break apart
into smaller pieces.

Did you know glaciers don't exist only at the poles? You can find them everywhere in the world.

Oh, what a sweet polar bear!

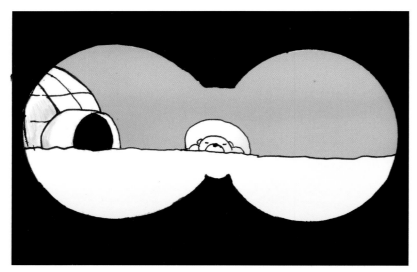

At the North Pole itself there are no humans, but on the land around it there are. Those people are called Inuit or Eskimos. They used to live in igloos made of ice. They wore animal skins and slept on them too. They made small holes in the ice to catch fish, hunted for food, and kept herds of reindeer.

Life at the poles

The North Pole ....

On an expedition to the poles

Did you know
there was a real race to be the first
to reach the poles? Explorers from
the United States, England and
Norway tried to be the first
ones to get there.

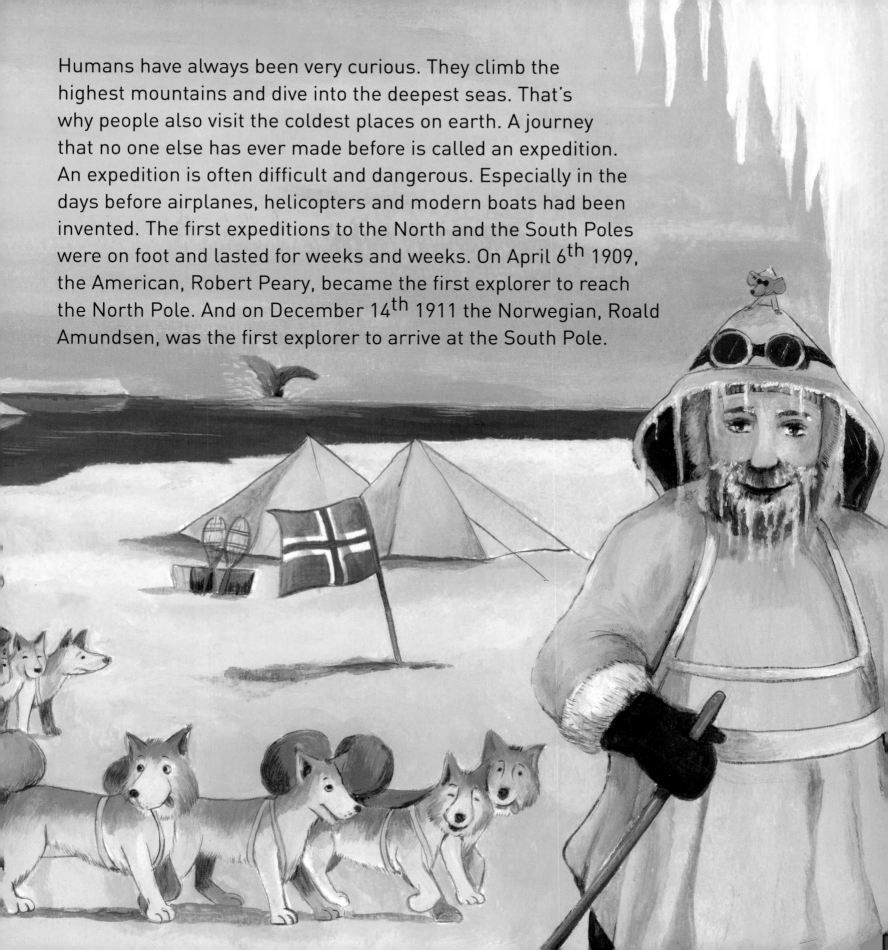

Humans have always been very curious. They climb the highest mountains and dive into the deepest seas. That's why people also visit the coldest places on earth. A journey that no one else has ever made before is called an expedition. An expedition is often difficult and dangerous. Especially in the days before airplanes, helicopters and modern boats had been invented. The first expeditions to the North and the South Poles were on foot and lasted for weeks and weeks. On April 6th 1909, the American, Robert Peary, became the first explorer to reach the North Pole. And on December 14th 1911 the Norwegian, Roald Amundsen, was the first explorer to arrive at the South Pole.

There are no humans living at the South Pole. It's far too cold. The people who are there only stay for a little while. Most of them are scientists doing research. They study the penguins, whales, and weather. They study ice, and check to see if it's melting.

They live in tents, cabins or modern labs and move about on snowmobiles or tracked vehicles. They bring all the supplies they might need with them from home, because they can't go shopping at the South Pole!

The South Pole

Did you know the word "igloo" means "house" in the language of the Inuit?

Modern Eskimos don't live in igloos. They live in houses made of wood or stone. They don't travel by dog sled anymore either, they get around using snowmobiles.

What happens if the ice melts?

Scientists say that the earth is slowly getting hotter. That is because there are many people on the earth who use lots of fuel and that is causing the earth's temperature to rise.

Scientists call it global warming and it might cause the ice to melt. Of course there is a lot of ice, and it will take a very long time for it to melt. If the ice melts, the water in all the seas will rise. It could rise so high that some streets, houses and cities will be under water.

The animals that live at the North or the South Poles cannot live anywhere else, and if they lose their homes, they will be endangered.

Did you know global warming is also called the greenhouse effect?

Penguins

The King Penguin

Penguins are birds that can't fly, but are excellent swimmers. There are seventeen different kinds of penguins. The Emperor Penguin is the best known. Penguins live both in the water and on the land. In the water they search for food – mostly fish, lobsters and small cephalopods. On the land they build nests, lay eggs and hatch them. Among most kinds of penguins, both parents take turns to keep the egg warm, and both parents take care of their young ones once the eggs have hatched. Among Emperor Penguins, only the male hatches the egg.

The Emperor Penguin

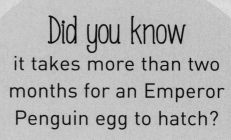

Did you know
it takes more than two months for an Emperor Penguin egg to hatch?

Did you know penguins don't live only at the South Pole? You can also find them in South America, South Africa, Australia and New Zealand.

The Gentoo Penguin

The Chinstrap Penguin

The Adélie Penguin

The Macaroni Penguin

Penguin Step

My class went to the zoo.
There was so much to learn and do.
Who knew that penguins never flew?

Standing around in their suits
they really do look very cute
until they start to walk –
we laughed so hard we couldn't talk!

"Let's walk like penguins!"
someone called.
And then we had a ball
doing the penguin step.
Doing the penguin step.

First you sway to the left, then you sway to the right.
You almost topple over, it gives you such a fright!
You wobble to the left, you wobble to the right.
It really is a funny sight:
You rock from foot to foot,
not walking at all,
you roll and you toddle
till you think you're going to fall.

But wait...

See the penguins in the water they don't look strange at all!
They're sleek and smooth and slick and slidy.
They swiftly slice through water icy.

In the Antarctic it's blustery, blowy, cold and snowy.
There the penguin rules!
Even though when he walks – he rocks!

What a beautiful Macaroni Penguin!

This is what you need:

an empty roll of toilet paper

white, orange and black paper (or paper that you've colored yourself)

black blotting paper

felt-tip pens and colored pencils

a newspaper

scissors

glue or sticky tape

This is what you do:

The body and the feet:

1. Fold a piece of orange letter size paper in two and cut it in half.
2. Fold one half in two and paint a little heart on it.
Cut out the heart shape. These will be the penguin's feet.

The face:

3. Cover the toilet paper rolls with white paper. This will be the penguin's body.
4. Stick the feet and the body together with glue.
5. Take a piece of newspaper and make it into a ball.
6. Cover the ball with black blotting paper. This will be the penguin's head.
7. Cut out two little circles from a white piece of paper and draw a dot in the middle of each circle. These will be the eyes.
8. Draw a circle on the remaining half of the orange paper.
Cut it out and cut it in half. Roll the semi-circle into a nice sharp beak and glue it onto the ball.
9. Glue the little eyes onto the face.
10. Cut small strips from the orange paper and glue it to the back of the head.

Body, face and wings:

11. Stick the head and body together.
12. Fold the black piece of paper into a triangle.
13. Glue the middle of the black triangle to the back of the body.
14. Fold the wings a few times and your Macaroni Penguin is ready!

So many beautiful animals!

How many animals do you see?

Answers

1. At the North Pole.

2. Antarctica.

3. No, you can also find them in other places in the world.

4. The greenhouse effect.

5. Seventeen.

6. Inuit.

7. No, there is water under the North Pole.

8. No, it's colder at the South Pole.

9. House.

10. At the South Pole.

Mini-quiz

1. Where do polar bears live?

2. What is another name for
   the South Pole?

3. Do glaciers exist only at the poles?

4. What is another way to say
   global warming?

5. How many different types
   of penguins are there?

6. What is another name for Eskimos?

7. Is there land underneath the North
   Pole?

8. Is it warmer at the South Pole
   than at the North Pole?

9. What does the word "igloo" mean
   in the Inuit language?

10. Where do penguins live?